Tincture

GW00724627

Tincture

Amy Phillips

Paper Doll

Published by Paper Doll
Belasis Hall
Coxwold Way
Billingham
Cleveland

ISBN: 1 86248 091 5

Typeset by CBS, Martlesham Heath,
Ipswich, Suffolk
Printed by Lintons Printers, Co. Durham

Contained within these pages is a selection of writing that spans nearly ten years.

I began to express myself verbally in my teens with the odd short verse and occasional poem but because I'd always considered my main form of expression was visual I often lacked confidence in my words.

As my health gradually deteriorated and the depression deepened I became blocked and could no longer create in any way. Time passed and eventually I found writing seemed to be my only outlet. Words would come in short, sharp bursts and the majority of what is written here is as I spewed it to the page, capturing the moment, the emotion, which is also why much of the work remains untitled. I have never deliberately sat down to write, it comes at the most unexpected moments.

For me this collection marks a journey through altering states of mind and spaces. It records experiences that are now merely stains and provides a memory of what I consider to be the most difficult and distressing period of my life.

WRITTEN IN THE PAST

(1989-1990)

Emptiness surrounds me like a shroud,
Empty friends, empty words,
False actions, painfully polite gestures,
Empty rooms echoing my sadness,
Hollow arms, hollow legs, hollow head,
This lethargy controls me.

* * *

Drowning in loneliness
My eyes no longer see the future.
All that's left is now,
slipping between my grasping fingers.
My water logged brain begins to drive me insane,
I spin like an object trapped in a whirlpool,
following its downward spiral.

AMY

Within this body is a mind so complex,
I don't even understand what I feel.
It contains thoughts and emotions
I can never release.

FELIX-TOW

You step back from your safe little routines.
No threats,
same people, same places.
One day I'll make the break.

SUNLESS SEDUCTION

The room spins violently,
an endless spiral.
Sanity suffers
Then succumbs to seduction,
The subtle allure of despair.

I scream wildly
The room now runs red
and blood flows freely.
The blade it weeps
while the heart wound seeps.

The room I'd had became a nightmare
where darkness hid creatures,
ones I'd created.
They beckoned me closer,
'Closer, closer!'
But I ran faster, faster,
hitting walls,
destroying the plaster.

My spirit remains
where I was once slaughtered
as blood flow still,
ingrained in floorboard.

BEWILDERED DISMEMBERMENT

That innocent girl you once thought you knew
was dragged screaming through youth,
plunged deep into a hellish ocean.
Tugged apart in selfish guilt.
Innocence lost untimely.
And no one knew, you never knew.

Hours I spent dumbly staring,
mirrored eyes, narrow, fixed.

Scissors pressed eagerly into my body,
and the waiting.
The warmth as the blood trickled
over my stomach, over and down my thighs.

Over and over
Tumbling through darkness.
The voices screeching, ripping to shreds,
I curled and cowered in the blood sodden bed.

Deceit and lies congeal in my mind
I want to strike out, dismember, destroy
To smash the illusions that surround me,
that crowd and smother,
'Til I see no way but down . . .
. . . down to receive the warmth of others.

I'll watch while you weep
with frustration and anger
The lack of understanding of the worlds
I was torn between.
One which held nothing, merely a book of days.
The other, unknown, yet enticing.

DON'T JONES ME

Hellish howls surround this space.
Bodies lying lifeless, restrained beneath
secured straps.
Naked, pale flesh conceals the true abuse.
Eyes bulging and restless,
trapped inside soulless sockets.
Blood gurgles from the nose and throat
of a carcass.

Lifelines thrust into throats,
force feeding the menu:
Chemical cocktails with a hint of pineapple
and listerine.

Changing of the seasons pass unnoticed
inside the hallucinogenic void.
Some have died while ceasing to exist.
A body but no brain to connect with.
They'll eagerly turn you off but rarely on.

Intoxicating, that smell muddles the memory.

QUILT HER

Petals wither and decompose amidst a mass of
decaying leaves,
blown from the branches of once vibrant trees
which are now skeletal forms,
piercing the atmosphere.
Obediently swaying.

Evenings spent imagining creatures appearing,
from the shadows of this once blossoming garden.

Shadowing figures dance and beckon me,
enticing and entrancing.
The glass falls,
smashing against the sill.
I fling open the window and fly.

* * *

From within the subconscious leaks poison.
Seeping,
mingling and mixing with the conscious.
It brings memories once forgotten.
Never whole,
merely sections, sentences, screams.
Confusing, absurd.

SLIGHT
(1994)

DIS/ORDER

Bingeing destroys the soul,
it leaves me feeling weak,
out of control.
Perverse sensations, a lustful greed.
Uncontrollable urges sweep through me
Eat, eat, fill, stuff, cram until it's all gone,
the loaf of bread, a jar of chocolate spread,
and that's just for starters.
Swig, eat, swig, eat and so it goes on
until my stomach is straining.
No more – it honestly can't take it
but still I continue in this orgy
sometimes to the point where,
if I have another mouthful,
I may be sick.
My stomach churns and gets bloated,
self inflicted pain.

This is why it has to stop.
I need to eat regularly, good food and be satisfied
instead of these frenzied feeds,
on foods that disagree with me.
Why do I do this?
I'm rarely hungry when I start, perhaps peckish,
maybe boredom.
I honestly couldn't say
But once I begin . . .
Oh what the hell, let's just go for it.

A continual struggle against the negativity which
restrains,
holds me back – hemmed in.
It creates irrational feelings
that cause you to fear
To keep you sealed inside a safe cocoon
Sabotaging till you shrink out of view.

* * *

Imagine, how it must feel to be
TRAPPED
Stuck inside this frail frame
Take 2 steps forward, 2 steps back
Never getting anywhere.

SOLO, SO LOW, SOL ARE

I stand in a queue, basket full of food
and people they stare.
I feel their eyes scanning my scrawny frame.
I return their stares with hard, fixed eyes.
'What's your problem?'
                                        I'd love to scream.
Sometimes I hear comments whispered as I pass.
I know what they think ANOREXIC.
When I'm happy and they stare I never care.
I walk tall ignoring it all.
But on tired days like these, standing here,
shoulders bare, shorts revealing limbs.
In a queue their eyes burn into me
and their thoughts,
sadden and anger.
I'm trapped at the check-out,
crouched on the floor,
weak, waiting, wishing.

MICKLEOVER MADNESS

(1995-1996)

My family is a unit of three.
First born and brother related to mother.
It's easy to know how far you can go,
within the bounds of expected normality.
But I broke the mould,
How far did I go?
Beyond the realm of living reality.
I became a ghost of myself,
trapped in a personal hell
that controlled each waking moment.
Try as I might, I just couldn't fight
and slowly began to wither.
My limbs got thinner
I began to dither.
Incontinence slowly crept in.
I floated around, feet skimming the ground
so no trace of my presence remained.

Why am I so scared of life?

* * *

I know it's there, waiting,
waiting to come back and get me
at the times I least expect.
But I still live in hope of being able to cope
and destroy doubts which linger and haunt me.
It was worth the fight.
I need a life.

The facade I've created, this mask of indifference
protects a frightened young girl underneath.
She's not sure about life, if she'll ever get it right
or even have the guts to begin it.
But you've seen through its cracking veneer
to the sickening sadness and potential madness,
once kept out of sight.

* * *

I get into bed and curl up tight
and while I pick at scabs I think.
Three scars on my right arm never heal,
their wounds reopened daily.
Now there's one on my shoulder
and as I get older
these distinguishing marks remain.

Then sometimes I fantasize about lovers
past and new,
deep down it feels so incredibly real
but I know it'll never be true.
So I'm here on my own, in this so called home
with only these arms for comfort.
As darkness surrounds I slowly drown
in the washing of conflicting voices.

When the pain comes, the panic spreads
Seeping into untamed thoughts,
plaguing me – constantly.
They're relentless waves disturbing reality,
Will I ever be free?

OSTEO

Bones are crunching,
clicking into place.
Discs slipping.
Severe sensations.
Spinal distress.

* * *

Breasts are forming.
Contours curving.
For the first time they're real.
Still no blood yet dripping.

* * *

What if I carried out my heart's desire,
to smash this glass in my hand.
In slow motion I see the image of fragments
and splinters,
showering the bed as I grab a handful and
squeeeeeze.

IN GRAIN

Scrapped out from within.
Its fingers grasp the inner tubes and grapple.
Now they're dug in and bloating,
bloating me out.
Pain on the left, the left, it's left,
and now on the right.
It's got me both sides.

* * *

Let me unleash this aggression I keep bubbling,
beneath the skin.
It's blistering out, forcing words to sting.
The physical reality of all this is far too scary
to consider.
If I let this free, the violence which follows
would overwhelm.
If I could hit, scream, punch, kick, shout,
spew it all out,
'til I'm left exhausted and weak.
A shell of myself.
The body is just a boundary, a border.

ROOM NEIN

So she became another name
on the psychiatrist's book.
In a room with blancmange coloured walls,
the radiators pump out warmth which escapes
through open windows.
Magazines sit in orderly piles daring the reader
to disturb the display.
Unnecessary lighting enhances this sterile scene.
Meanwhile I swallow a sickening in my throat.
If this is meant to make you feel at ease then . . .

Then I'm caught scribbling these notes
by a frumpy woman in specks.
'AMY PHILLIPS.'
'Yes,' I promptly reply, mid-sentence.
'Come this way.'
So obediently I get up and follow her into a room.
It's pink too with several chairs, a pristine mirror
and a sink I could use as a loo.

She attracts my gaze,
attempting to focus my attention.
Her frizzy, distressed split ends irritate.
That dull dress of green hiding any possible shape.
To me, she is just a mass of flesh.

I can see her looking at me,
searching
for a deeper meaning to my words.
Are they truth or lies?
Only I know but I'm not so sure.
I return the stare and sit there intent
on deluding her.

But it's all a joke.
There are no pills for her to ram down my throat
which is obviously her first line of thought.
So in the end I leave, pissed off but appeased.
If this is psychotherapy then there is no hope.

Sarah is screaming.
Hyped as a fuck.
Her eyes are now slits, seeing stains,
seeing smears.
A memory maimed.
Secretly shredded.
Internal lies torturing.

Coughing up her guts
Sinister sounds spewing screams.
It travels up through the ceiling,
this onslaught of words.
Then there's Rob, who's in there also,
as always, trying to keep her sane.

Lying still I listen.
A momentary lull.
I relax.
Then she starts again.
Hideous hacking, forcing out hatred.
Choking on pain again and again.
The tension remains.

* * *

Sounds through the walls remind you of home.
Fucked up voices screaming their pain.
Frustrated fists.
You're fighting the fear.

SUMMER – LOST
(1996)

FROM-ARGE

You suck me dry.
Like pumice I grate,
scratching the skin, exposing cells.
I'll rub you up the wrong way,
just like an old cliché.

You're the cheese guy
Edam man
who drives me mad like no other one can.
The stifling smell of sickness
Texture of rubber,
makes me wonder
How you can put it in your mouth.

A voice cracked over the phone.
Indistinguishable words became audible.
My senses are alerted to all the sounds.
What was that she said?
'He's in intensive care.'
She sounded fragile.
I should have picked up the phone.
Instead I let her think I wasn't here,
but I am, listening in.
I can't face the thought of talking.
Not to you,
not to anyone.

These are strange emotions to feel
for someone I barely know.
The few times we've met
his presence has overwhelmed.
I want to see him even though
there'd be no recognition.
He's beyond that now,
unable to survive without the ventilator.
His heart can't cope alone anymore.
On release he relapses.

TRIANGLE OF SCARS SHOWS ME
WHO YOU ARE
THEY'RE REMINDERS OF
THE SELF ABUSE
THE MUTILATION

'WISHING'

A SERIES OF BRUISES
ENTRAP AND FORM
IT GIVES ME AN INSIGHT

'THE SUBCONSCIOUS LIES'

NO LONGER SEEING PAIN
INSTEAD I GAIN GROUND
MOVE ON
DISCARDING THE PAST

'TO EMBRACE'

NO MORE EMBRYONIC EXISTENCES
OR
FOETAL FRUSTRATIONS

'I GLIDE'

Yellow beaded heart and slender
white laced limbs,
You shine your light on everything
So tender, so blind and oblivious to me.

The breeze blows and disturbs
those resting moments when
you shine your light on everything but
you're purely just for me.

Now you're limp and fading,
I wish you wouldn't go.
But gorgeous flower it's my fault,
I should have left you alone.

I MUST LUST RAL

MY HEAD IS LEFT MID SPACE
THIS LUSTRAL TO GIVE ME
LUST FOR LIFE
HAS LEFT ME DEAD.
FEEL NO SORROW
FEEL NO PAIN
NO DESIRE . . .

ALL THIS BANISHED TO QUELL
THE LONGINGS,
THE NEED TO EXPRESS,
EXPERIMENT AND FULFIL
TO QUENCH THE FRUSTRATIONS
THAT DRAIN
AND HOLD ME IN TORMENT.
WHEN ALL DISTRACTIONS ARE GONE
AND ONCE AGAIN
I AM ALONE.

AUGUST

I'm hibernating,
sleeping as long as I wake.
This weight loss doesn't make me feel better.
I've watched it drop and it's scaring
to see this return.
It's a vicious circle.
The more I sleep the less I eat.
The less I eat, the less I do and collapse
back into bed.
THESE TABLETS CALM,
DISARM
AND DRAIN.

Teeth Gripping,
Ripping Up Your Flesh
Dragging Back The Cells
Until You're Under My Skin.
I'll Cling On And Draw Blood.

BOULD-ER

Zipped shut
teeth as stone
Lips bursting to speak
but no words released.

*   *   *

A SHRINK WRAPPED MASS OF LIMBS,
GROWING THIN.
TRANSLUCENT FLESH AND VEINS
SO DELICATE.

The mirror reflects back at me
a sight I do not want to see,
panda eyes and bruised lips.
Ugliness.

This self hatred colours all perception.
I'm left seeing lies, illusions
created inside to make me hide
when I'm not strong enough to fight.

Sometimes it's hard to see
when your eyes are the size of peas.

RIDICULOUS RHYMES
(1997)

A day in Dallinghoo drifts by,
just the dog and I.
We potter and pace around the house,
remaining silent,
voicing doubts,
about the way life should be led
and sometimes I just wish for bed
but unlike our dog I can't justify
these movements circular and uninspired.

PREFORM – A

Chicken? Ham? Or was it spam,
who can tell the difference anyway.
It's all remains and flesh,
moulded and packaged,
sweaty cellophane
see through veins,
ventricles emerge wafer thin
or languish inside a tin.
Chicken? Ham?
When all I want is strawberry jam.

SEVEN ELEVEN

They said,
'Six sizzling sausages sat sizzling in a pan.'
I NEVER COULD.
(they said) 'Save our seals.'
I NEVER WOULD . . .
but at night I sometimes tried as I laid there
and cried
repeating these rhymes.
Desperate and tired,
through a lisping tongue these words stung.

Rain splatters on the pane
It sounds so loud it hurts my brain
and the system's pumping hot and cold
I hear it bubble, hiss and clank
the metal piping near the tank.

Draughts they whistle round my head
So I curl up tight beneath the bed
But still they find me clutching bone
as I rest upon the telephone.

And the TV's talking to itself
as I wonder if you've ever felt
The urge to melt into the floor
and leave a stain,
forever more.

DERWENT

There was a young duck called Dillon
whose coat was bright green and vermillion.
His favourite tea was Lapschong shu
which he sipped through a straw,
striped with blue.

He couldn't fly and couldn't swim
so he sat on the floor with a curious grin.
Seasons changed and still he stared
at the others who flew by without a care.

TOUL-OUSE

Toulouse Lautrec was a very nice man
who painted on canvas
with a brush in one hand,
in the other he held a bottle of stout
which he drank divinely while eating trout.
The dancing girls and scenes of bars
only made enough to buy him a car.
Whereupon he raced about till
he met his end on a dangerous bend.
Trout in his ear, stout down his front
and a brush stuck firmly right up his trunk.

TOUL-OUSE Mk 2

Toulouse Lautrec was a very nice man
who painted on canvas
with a brush in one hand,
in the other he held a bottle of stout
which he drank divinely while eating trout.
The dancing girls and scenes of bars
only made enough to buy him a car.
He raced around the countryside
till he reached the day he finally died.
They never did know how to get it out,
that brush jammed firmly up his snout.

Nail varnish that's blue and sticks like glue,
the tongue out of my head
to the corner of the bed,
a finger to my thigh and another to my eye.
I should have chosen red
as it resembles meat spread,
the way it coats the nail
and leaves a blood like trail.

HOO

Through dusky hues silhouettes loom.
Pylons piled high.
Steel wrecks scarring skies.
Humming wires,
taut and stunning
pigeons mid flight.
Feathers singed and bodies burnt
they rot below in electrified earth.

* * *

Anxiety states make for nervous mistakes.
Dishonesty causes confusion.
I'm dying from within.

SKIDDAW

Self confidence at an all time low.
Appearance, its importance underlined
has served to undermine . . . ability.
Now I see an ugly duckling staring back at me.
Quack,
    Quack, Quack
    Quackers
    Quacked

Then there's the hammering,
chalet shaking thunder and white lightning.
Plucked guitar strings, song repetition
they're like goldfish trapped inside this bowl.
How I wish I was a fish with a memory span
that would allow me to
. . . forget not regret the wasted time.
Noise would annoy then I'd realise again,
then I'd realise again
this will never end.

RETURNING
(1998)

PRIORY

They've washed away my blood, its stains,
yet streaks of sick and the stench remains.
While cold and tired I think of death
Sterile and surrounded
Wipe out, white out.
Still the sheen of the sink
and smell of soap reminds me
I still have some hope.
Searching for warmth inside and out
I'll bleach away life,
they'll bleach away death.

So suspended held and apart
I leap directly in the bath
surrounded by steam,
deflecting the gleam.
Drink the water
cup after cup
then I'll turn blue with a razor's cut.

Lips sucking on the painted sill,
sucking so hard I feel quite ill.
My need for air gone to extremes,
if I don't breathe soon I'm going to scream.
Instead there's a warmth,
it's stifling,
dulling the senses,
making me stupid and caged
desperation has set in.
Need sunlight and skies,
want freedom and life
when all I have is just one inch.

OVARIES
WOMB
RED
TESTICLES
THIGHS
FLUID
PENIS
PAIN
CONDOM
STERILE
SCARRED

NOV, EMBER

I lie awake in the half light with wandering eyes
and a head full of sins with nowhere to begin
and the urge to run, to find someone
to live without the need for a knife.
KNIFED again
and I refrain from detailing pain,
to empty ears I'm recalling fears
that rewind and replay most everyday.
Snatched moments, lost words
that'll never be heard.
KNIFED again
bottle burning the skin, leaving scars.
I remove and replace
clutching, curling tightly in vain
but the tension remains.

VI-O-LEN-C

Cruel in body, cruel in mind
I was certainly never that kind,
the violence I craved came from within.
Spiteful words, a vicious tongue licked
'You're useless, pathetic
and don't count for shit.'
Battered, bruised, pale and blue,
lips bleeding and bitten from being so chewed.

Tired, pained and totally drained
I lie inert, surrounded by dirt.
Head swimming, eyes skimming
the creases and folds of covers curled tight
while I pray for night
but even in sleep I still can't find peace.

EMILY

Emily, your strength remains,
your spirit so powerful and strange.
Full of life and fresh in youth,
your beauty came from being you.
I loved you in a quiet way
and miss you dearly everyday.
You called me just before you died,
perhaps you knew,
I can't decide.
To face the truth tore me apart
and the pain it stung me deep in the heart
but I've had to let it go a little,
not cling to the anger that made me so brittle
as I'd snap at the mention of your name
and return to the memories of that day.
Tears would come and I'd curl up small,
crying endless sorrow in a caterwaul.

MAROONED

The baby that grew inside of you,
created feelings so new.
Even while forming,
still foetal and feeding
you had a place for it in your plans,
that bulge you cradled in your hands.
Barely showing,
I saw you glowing
with an unborn knowing.

AFTERMATH

A gaping wound remained inside,
a space to fill too deep to hide,
aching and empty with no flap of skin
to conceal and cover,
Where do I begin?

The hollowness was part of life,
a reminder of forgotten things.
Confusion when and if it did arise
was swallowed safely out of sight
and sucked in tight
to rebound once more off internal walls
that supported her structure,
kept her tall.
Without them she might fall apart
and risk revealing
a bruised and bloodied heart.

There were things she craved,
just to be loved,
to be tender and held,
not solitary and hard.

Brushing away the past,
disregarding rape
but the scars hadn't really healed at all,
to still dream of it,
it could always happen again and again,
sometimes those nightmares never seemed to end.

A blunted blade held to the throat,
soiled mattresses bound in rope.
There were two,
no three of us,
maybe even four
but I always managed
to jolt awake seconds before.

I'd say to the girl beside me,
'Don't fight it, it'll make it worse,
lie back corpse like,
be lifeless,
pretend you're just a whore,
you are the victim being used
but maybe then you'll be excused
and learn to deal with the disgrace
in your own silent, secret way
until it all becomes too much one day.'

The damage done can be repaired
yet I remain forever scared
of being touched in a physical way
even by those I love
and who mean no harm,
that feeling I just can't disarm.

The fear is always in my mind
and I wish I had the time
to find someone
willing to help me come undone.

I cannot touch you
yet I want to try,
I need the love
that you deny.